THE STREETS, LIKE FLOWERS, COME ALIVE IN THE RAIN

Steve Denehan

The Streets, Like Flowers, Come Alive in the Rain

Reprinted by **Baxter House Editions**: www.darkwinterlit.com

Artwork by Steve Denehan

The following poems first appeared in:
The Grass was Long and Soft & U-Turn - Capsule Stories
Surface Tension - Tinfish Press
She Calls it My Pinkie Fingernail - Placeholder Press
Spiders Have Eight Eyes - The Ogham Stone
Watching a French Film in a Dublin Cinema, Twelve Years Ago - Selcouth Station
London, Seagulls and Silence & Glass Bottom - Ice Floe Press
Simmering - Fevers of the Mind
Vegetables and Iron - Kansas City Voices

ISBN: 978-1-7382734-8-5

Steve Denehan
www.stevedenehan.wixsite.com/website

For my family and friends and for Suzanne, for taking a chance

CONTENTS

FOREWORD

My name is Robin, and I am eight years old. My Dad wrote this book. He writes poems every day, and it is exciting to see some of them in a book. Some of his poems are funny, and some are sad, and some are about our family. Once, he came into my class to talk about writing, and I was very proud. His poems always make me think. It is nice when I read about myself in his poems because I remember all of the funny things. It is really nice to read about myself when I was a baby because I don't remember those times at all. I also like to read about when he was younger because I like knowing more about him. My favourite poem in this book is called "One More Week." My Dad is a very good Dad.

~Robin Denehan

A RAINY NIGHT ON WEXFORD STREET, DUBLIN

I sit in a Dublin café amongst other stragglers
it is cold
it is rainy
condensation beads on the windowpane
droplets snake down and puddle on the tabletop
I pierce meniscuses with a toothpick
there is a bang outside
not too loud
but loud enough for everyone inside
to turn, to look

one car has driven into the back of another
several perfect moments of utter stillness drip by
before the car doors open
a man emerges from the first
a woman from the second
the man points his finger at her
I hear him fling words
the woman puts her hands on her head
starts to cry

I look away
to see what Dublin makes of it all
some people stare
most just walk on by
heads down
earphones in
it takes less than one half minute
for the backed-up traffic horns
to start to blare

when I look back
they are standing beside their jigsawed cars
he is holding her in his arms
she is heaving with sobs
I see puddles ripple with neon
and understand that the streets
like flowers
come alive in the rain

TRIP TO PORTUGAL, SUMMER, 2016

We could see the heat out of the small window
but couldn't feel it yet
we remained in our seats
watching the rest of the passengers
stampede slowly past
their hurry to rush off the plane, into the airport
only to wait
again
for their luggage
always baffled

we thanked the cabin crew
stepped out of the door
stood at the top of the stairs
felt the punch of the heat
a soft hammer blow
looked at the rippling brightness of it all
smiled at each other

we walked through the airport
queued with the rest

had our passports stamped
joined the other passengers
waiting by the empty baggage carousel
some, paced up and down
willing their luggage to appear

we sat, stretched out
breathed in the heat
my daughter pointed to an airport policeman
he was carrying a gun
she had never seen a gun before
not in real life
she asked me why
they would need guns here
in all of this sunshine
it was a good question

ONE TENTH OF A SECOND

It seemed to materialise in my rear-view mirror
a black Audi
silver trim
so close that I couldn't see the reg
or the headlights
or half of the bonnet

I could see him clearly
hunched toward the steering wheel
short black hair
intense, unblinking eyes
straight-line mouth
maybe half my age

there were cars in front
cars to the side
nowhere for me to go
he flashed his lights nonetheless
through sheer tyranny of will
I tried, and failed, to evaporate

I touched the brakes
silent, screaming fury in the rear-view mirror
he pulled back to a safer distance
for five seconds or so
before roaring up behind me
furiously, again

I almost admired his determination
to get where he was going
one tenth of a second quicker
I wanted to ask him why, just why
I wanted to put his hand in a woodchipper
and watch the rest of him follow

turned out our destination was the same
and for all his tailgating
both of us arrived at Liffey Valley Shopping Centre
at exactly the same time
actually, that's not entirely accurate
I won, by one tenth of a second

A PHONE CALL FROM MORGAN FREEMAN ON CHRISTMAS EVE

His name was Arndt
he was bald and squat
we sat in a Dublin pub one Christmas Eve
I didn't want to be there
he had nowhere else to be
my colleagues buzzed around
clinking and drinking
company Christmas bonding
a waking nightmare

Arndt, like me, was a programmer
the company had flown him in
money-no-object
with a yearend deadline looming
to fix some code
he was the only person on the planet that could
as he had written it
decades before
when he had worked for Microsoft

Arndt sat in a Hawaiian shirt
out of place but easy in himself
we got to talking
an unassuming guy
even as his tales got taller

I asked about the shirt
he said that he had got the call and came
in the clothes that he was wearing
straight from Bermuda
I got his life story
or the highlights
of which there were many
from his Microsoft days
how he had been there at the beginning
had bought some shares
and then some more
and some more after that

born in America, raised in China
he trained in martial arts and co-ran a dojo
with Steven Seagal
I tried to picture him in his karate gear
jumping and chopping
this barrel of a man
twenty years older
at least
than myself
after some years he returned to America
bought a glider

something to do
nothing beat it he said
he found another kind of silence up there
and eventually, he got the call
the American National Gliding Team were short
Arndt was in
there was a competition in Germany
I don't know how it was judged
how the winner was determined
but Arndt leaned towards me
tilted his phone
and I saw him, younger
in red, white and blue
holding a gold medal

he cashed in some of his shares
bought some land near Vegas
on a whim
put a shooting range on it
spent a lot of time with a gun in his hand
found that he had a knack for it
that he could hit a target from half a mile away
then put another bullet through the same hole
without it touching the sides

with time, he opened it up to the public
hired some teachers
trained some bodyguards, military, CIA specialists
was noticed by another sharpshooter
went on to represent his country again

this time at the Olympics

he had been shot twice
I didn't ask him to show me his scars
and he didn't offer
but he didn't like it
getting shot
so, he put the guns down

Arndt was idle
a regular from the shooting range noticed
offered him a huge sum to transport
just a little uranium
by land
to
with a wink
somewhere
bored, Arndt took the job
bought a Harley
drove the uranium across America
saw the sites and got a tan
while the dollars kept on rolling in

when he turned fifty, he covered his eyes
threw a dart at a map
landed in Australia the next day
for a few weeks
that became a few years
he bought an apartment that overlooked Sydney Opera House
saw the New Year fireworks from his balcony

drifted off most nights to symphonies
played by the world's greatest orchestras

his neighbour was Angus Young
from AC/DC
they went fishing together
on Angus' yacht
Arndt liked it
bought one just the same
pointed it at the horizon one day
and set sail

twelve days later the yacht was moored in Bermuda
the sun was low and Arndt sucked on cold beers
whilst being hypnotised by the cricket
on the television
in the small harbour bar
he got to talking with an old guy
turned out their yachts were moored side by side
turned out this old guy was at a loose end
having been kicked out by his wife
turned out this old guy had nowhere to be and nothing to do
but watch the cricket, sucking on beers
under the low sun
with Arndt
turned out this old guy was Morgan Freeman

I shook my head
found myself laughing
I put my hand on Arndt's shoulder

he looked at me
a little puzzled
a little sheepish

before I could speak
his phone rang from the bar
we looked at it
there was no number, just a name
Morgan
Arndt told me that he would let it go
call him back later
I told him to take it
take it
take it
I picked up the phone
handed it to him
he put it to his ear
answered it

Hey Morgan.
I'm good, I'm good.
Nah I'm in Dublin, yeah, Dublin, Ireland.
A bit of work. No, not that. A little coding.
Computer stuff, computer stuff.
Yeah, I'll be back in a week or so, keep my seat warm.
Happy Christmas to you too, keep an eye on my yacht.

through the satellite miles
and the small phone speaker
I heard it

that voice, sawdust and honey
the voice that God would have, should have
Arndt hung it up
put the phone back down on the table
asked me
to tell him
about myself
I hadn't got a thing to say

LITTLE GIRL IN THE HOTEL BAR

Her parents and another couple were talking loudly
had been for a while
the little girl sat patiently
playing with a beer mat
for a long, thin hour

eventually, she stood up
paused for a moment
as if expecting to be told
to sit back down
before walking to a panoramic window

she looked at the seagulls for a minute
but I knew that they held little interest for her
that she had really made her way to the window
to be close to *it*
the grand piano

it was immaculate, framed perfectly in the window
the keys, pure white, pure black
magnetic, irresistible

she looked around, slinked over
her hip against the piano side

I watched her finger move toward a key
while she looked the other way
it found the key bed
crept across it slowly
an intrepid inchworm

she pressed the key gently
held it down
that one note, a song
that waltzed across the hotel bar
to reach her parents

an argument ensued
they told her to stop
she asked them why she did the lessons at all
if she was never allowed to play
her father glared at her

I wondered what made their noise
more important than hers
after all, there were only beer mats for her here
I opened my face to him
suggested that maybe she could play a while

he looked at me
and without saying a word
told me that it was none of my business

before conceding
and nodding to his daughter

she grew an inch before us
cracked her fingers
sat down
surveyed the keys
a young old master

she looked at me
her eyes were summer lakes
her smile, the sky
her fingers, elegant, sure
and ready

she took a breath
closed her eyes
started to play
and frankly
she wasn't great

THE DESERT

We sat in the back of a jeep
somewhere in Morocco
having booked a day trip to the Sahara Desert
that morning a driver had collected us
he had very little English
we had been driving for three hours
I had expected there to be lots of sand
there was

I didn't see the point of driving any further
there was sand and only sand
before us
behind us
all around us
it was fifty degrees
the air was broken glass and sandpaper
we kept driving

I tapped the driver on the shoulder
told him that it was okay
that we could go back now
that we had seen the desert
he smiled and nodded

said, "Yes, yes!"
enthusiastically
and kept on driving

eventually, he stopped the jeep
got out, stretched
my wife and I looked at each other, shrugged and followed
the driver stood in front of us
closed his eyes
tilted his chin upward
held out his arms and exclaimed
The desert!

blue above us
yellow everywhere else
a caravan of camels
rippling in the distance
on the crest of a dune
stop-motion walking
moving almost imperceptibly
knots in a rope

THE TOSSED COINS OF JOHN CANNING

My wife and daughter stopped for pizza today
got talking to a guy outside
a drinker
mid-sixties
homeless
a hard life behind him
a harder one to come

he told them that he was a poet
that he was on YouTube
scrawled the details on an old cigarette box
his offering
handed over
with the hope that they would watch

my daughter told me later
that he had a kind face
that she wanted to tell him about me
before remembering that I had told her
I was not a poet
not really

so, she was silent

now I sit and think about him
the man and poet
of wrong turns
and bad calls
the man and poet
that tossed his coin and lost
more often than not

I sit, warm, in my home
my well-fed cat on the windowsill
the sky is blue but the sun is cold
I open YouTube, find him
I am not a poet but I know
that it could have been me
could still be yet

THE GRASS WAS LONG AND SOFT

The world is smaller now
because I make it small
but back then
at thirteen
on a late summer Saturday
it was infinite
a never ending
forever thing

except that
my knocks went unanswered
or were met with mothers' faces
telling me that Bob was sick
that Damien was not around
that Maura was off with her father
on that late summer Saturday
it was just me

I walked
down to the pinkeen pond
but the older boys were there

and one of them had destroyed my new bike that summer
for no reason at all
(fifteen years later, blind drunk
he would crash into my parked car
writing it off
what a guy)

I walked the couple of miles to the cinema
but there was nothing showing
nothing good at least
I got a bag of chips
extra salt
extra vinegar
extra crispy bits

arrived back at the green
sure, that there would be a match
a game of some sort
it was empty
but the grass was long and soft
and felt just fine when I laid upon it
put my feet up on the low wall
and watched the sky
and I think that that was the first time
I knew
really knew
I was going to be alright

THE CAR PARK

She used to ask me why we wait
she doesn't anymore
I collect her at the school gate
we walk to the car
I listen to her exclaim her news
"I tried an orange!"
"I learned about the coronavirus!"
"My new gloves are so snuggy!"

we are in no hurry
get into the car
turn on the music
wait
watch
the other cars jostle and funnel
toward the car park exit

we know them all by now
the cars
the people in them
the pantomime of it
forced smiles and white knuckles
it is our soap opera

it is our sitcom

we speculate on who will let who out
some people are polite
some are not
to some it's a war
a small, pathetic war
we watch them leave, all of them
hurriedly scuttling off
to do whatever it is that they do

she smiles at me in the rear-view mirror
I roll my eyes until only the whites show
she punches my shoulder
we get moving but I slam my foot on the brakes
jolting her forward
she punches my shoulder again
looks away from me in feigned disgust
in the empty car park
I put my foot down
race into a spiral
her laughter pours out our open windows
to corkscrew around the church spire
up and up and up

WOULDN'T IT BE NICE

The Beach Boys thought
it would be nice
if they were older
then they wouldn't have to wait so long

and these days it is us
who say a little prayer for
and to
Aretha

John Lennon no longer has to imagine
that there's no heaven
no hell below us

we all know what's gone before
we surely know what's coming
and still
we waste
the space
between

I mean
in the end
even Houdini
discovered
how to really disappear

HAVE A NICE DAY

She holds it out to me
while looking the other way
a receipt that belonged to the previous customer
I take it all the same
say *thanks* with a chuckle
she looks at me
understands
smiles tiredly
starts ringing in my groceries

she is good and the groceries come quickly
I put them in my bags
I have a system
hard in one bag
soft in the other
but my system goes out the window
in my hurry to keep up

I pay in cash
she hands me my change
never looking at me once
absentmindedly she says
Have a nice day

in the same way
that they all say it

unconsciously
like swatting a fly
or popping a blackhead
they never mean it
not really
and so, I always make
a silent promise to myself
to have a nice day
just to spite them

NECTAR

We enjoyed the slowness
how the days emerged softly
daylight gently filling the space
that the night had left behind
we enjoyed the mornings
late and long
the quiet midday breakfasts

we enjoyed the emptiness
wallowed in the time between the ticks and tocks
watched the clouds breeze by
found ourselves in them
prickling grass brushing our necks
enjoyed the sipping and savouring
the nectar of it all on our lips

then, with a small scream and sticky blinks, she came
we swaddled and bathed
rocked and hummed
followed and danced and laughed
through mouthfuls of popcorn

she came
and the days caught fire
flared across the sky
and we never once looked up

A SLOW DAY AT THE CAFÉ

The waitress was called Nancy
she was short and round and moved between us in flat shoes
us, was me, an old man who looked wistfully out of a window
and two young men sitting together
a slow day at the café

their voices were permanently raised
they seemed to have a lot to say
the noise from their chair legs caused vibrations in the air
they slurped and stirred and clinked
the alpha pounded the small table with his fist

the mugs and condiments jumped, landing with a clatter
Nancy respectfully asked them to keep it down
they laughed in her face
called her "Nance," laughed again
as she walked away, shorter and rounder

I stared at one of them
angled my knife slightly
watched a slice of sunlight

land across his throat
I held it there

they left before me
screeched away in a white Volkswagen Golf
Nancy mopped up their spills
stooped to pick up their discarded sugar packets
I left her a good tip

half an hour later I came upon the wreck
blue flashing lights, medics looking solemn
police waving us on, nothing to see here
alive or dead, I didn't know
I put my foot down and drove on towards the weekend

TENACIOUS D, FEBRUARY 10TH, 2020

The queue seemed to lengthen
the longer we were in it
shivering, we shuffled forward
smiling in the twinkling winter

it was her first big arena show
13,000 people and us
I saw her eyes wide open
I saw her eyes squeeze shut
locking in memories

the lights dimmed
the band came onstage
she, trembling before a note was played
us, looking down at her
trembling ourselves

the music came in a torrent
drowning her instantly, blissfully
we were happily forgotten
for two glorious hours

but I didn't forget you
you were there with me
and not at home
fading, gently
you were there with me Dad
just like I was there with you
this month, in 1957
at the Theatre Royal in Dublin
to see Bill Haley and his Comets
twenty years before I was born

how the music ran from you
to me
to her
how it will run after you
and me
and her

you were there with me
maybe for the last time
for her first time
it was something
wasn't it?

SLAM

The photograph on the wall
a timestamp, perfect, almost
one of the good days

when she walked out, she slammed the door
I mean, she really slammed it
the photograph shook
I thought it might fall
it didn't

I can see it from where I sit
think, that I really must straighten it
so, I do and then
it really is over
and I realise
that the problem
is not that things end
but that they continue

UNICORN DRESSING GOWN

Only occasionally do I hurt her
when I brush her hair
the trick is to hold a section
tightly, near the scalp
before quickly brushing the knots away

she used to sit on my lap for the brushing
now, she is a big girl
eight-years-old and tall with it
nowadays she sits beside me
in her unicorn dressing gown

So soft, feel it Dad
and I do, and it is
but soon unicorn dressing gown will be cast aside
the way of many other things
soon
she will brush her own hair

THE DILIGENT GOLDFISH-SITTER

We lived five minutes from the airport
our childhood skies were vapour trails
and thundering, sun kissed engines

we visited the airport on Sunday afternoons
to gaze at the planes, and imagine
with our feet planted firmly on the ground

my friend casually told me
that his family were flying to France
he asked me to mind his goldfish

the next day I looked up
wondered which plane he was on
while his goldfish swam in a small bowl in our kitchen

I was a diligent goldfish-sitter
fed him a little, three times a day
talked to him, when no one could hear

I watched him swim back and forth
around and around
I tapped on the glass but he never responded

sometimes the sun would catch his scales
and he would become a magical thing
almost holy

other times I would stare into his eyes
to find nothing
the eyes flat and dead and joyless

we came home one afternoon to find him
dry and lifeless on the kitchen floor
I had forgotten to put the lid on the bowl

my father was furious, at first
before bundling us back into the car
our mission, top secret, to replace the goldfish

a week later my friend returned
I handed him the bowl
the imposter went unnoticed

another week passed
I heard how frog's legs taste like chicken
and how ears pop on an airplane

how it doesn't feel that fast when you are up there
how the clouds look the same above, as below

how it was quite boring, overall

I listened, but all the while I thought of the lie
of my father flushing it down the toilet
how I couldn't even take care of a goldfish

another week went by
longer still, than the one before
the lie wriggled in between my ribs

I told him in the end, I had to
he looked at me, his eyes flat and dead and joyless
he didn't give a damn

THE FREE PEN

Usually, the storms have common names
almost bland, Brendan, Ciara
Dennis for Christ's sake
I don't know who christens the storms
but they loosened their collar for this one
Storm Jorge
a suntanned storm with mirror-shades
and a straw trilby, is what I imagined
instead, it is wilder and angrier than the rest
so, I sit inside watching the snooker
letting Jorge rage himself to a standstill

in between frames
an ad comes on
two people are talking
they are worried
clearly troubled
a disembodied voice tells them to worry no more
that they can cover their own funeral expenses
and put aside a little something for their family
simply by calling the number onscreen

they are an older couple
sitting in a pristine room
in pristine clothes
with pristine smiles
supposedly happy together
even though their conversation
is overly polite
stilted
as though they have just met
they ask blatantly obvious questions
are utterly amazed at the answers

they learn that there is a free pen for signing up
they look absolutely fucking delighted
at the very idea
of a free pen
I assume that it will be shared between them
the ad finishes with a quick run through of the terms and conditions
somewhere in the speech I hear
"in the event of your death"
they are still smiling
hard as they can
though their eyes are flat and joyless and I realise
that the ad is wasted on them
that the couple cannot die
having never lived

PEOPLE

I don’t hate all people
just most of them
after all, what is not to hate
selfies, simpering and small talk
nope

for a knock on the door
I freeze
(they can sense movement)
even hold my breath
(they can hear the heartbeats of a gnat)
until the footsteps dissolve into silence

when the phone rings
I roll under the table
and cover my ears
until the ringing stops

they get the message
eventually
now, there are no knocks
now, the phone doesn't ring
victory
I think

CURTAINS

You see yourself in the bathroom mirror
wonder if your dull skin, dull hair and dull eyes
are the result of the dull mirror light
you remember late night arm wrestling
pool tournaments
the crack of the balls
watery laughter

you remember when your joints didn't sing
when the world was too small, was yours
when sparks sprung from your fingertips
and fire from your mouth
when everything was fast
and still not fast enough
when the future was tomorrow

you're already missing summer
though the spring is yet to come
and in bed you lie and face the curtains
the night, and other things
behind them
and you leave them there
unforgotten and forgiven

TEETH

I went to strip her bed
to wash her sheets
first, I had to remove teddy bears
toys, so many

a teddy bear, soft and cute but
squeeze his belly and teeth are bared
jagged, sharp and snarling
a gossamer-winged fairy
a Rubik's Cube, two books
some pens and Batgirl, tucked beneath a blanket
knitted by a faraway friend

my arms half full, the bed half empty
I hear the door creak behind me
"What are you doing Dad!"
"I am washing your sheets."
"But it took me ages to get them comfy."
"I am sure the fresh sheets will be just as comfy."
"You are holding Batgirl by her head!"

I give her a look, our look
she knows, tries not to laugh

laughs anyway
I have her windows open a little
the room, not large enough
for the love that I can see
pouring through the slits
weaving between the tree branches
carrying birds and butterflies

"Am I too old to sleep with teddies Dad?"
"No way! Never!"
"Why don't you sleep with teddies anymore then?"
"Things change."
"I wish they didn't."
I smiled, hugged her
me too

RAIN

Happiness comes easy these days
I looked for it for decades
only to find that it was there all along
hiding in plain sight
in the folds of that old woollen blanket
in the press filled with lunchboxes and Tupperware
more than any family could ever use

even in the sheeting rain
rain that bounces up from the path as if boiling
rain that will fall forever
whatever “forever” means

rain that will fall
when all that remains of our happiness
can hide in that crack
in the grout
between our rust-coloured bathroom tiles

rain that will fall
long after we have

COBWEB SILK

They come away from him easily now
peels of paint from an accelerating car
a car picking up pace
with each passing day

the points of clock hands
pressing gently
the trembling memory meniscus
the agonising slow burst

he had heard the word 'meniscus' that morning
for the first time
in his eighty-two years
liked the sound of it, the feel of it

liked to think that water had a skin
wondered if it could be tattooed
bruised invisibly, cut
and stitched back together with cobweb silk

I enjoyed his brilliant mind before
five minutes later
meniscus
and other words
were gone

THE MIDDLE OF THE MIDDLE OF NOWHERE

The road was empty
a small road off a small road
lost, trying to go back the way I had come
I misjudged a three-point turn
felt my rear wheels slip
waited, as the car slowly eased back
halfway into a shallow ditch
twenty long minutes passed
no cars did

I started walking
and walking
toward nothing but the evening
I came upon a house
overgrown and sprawling
my knock went unanswered
for a while
but, there was shuffling inside
I waited

his skin was almost translucent
the slice of it visible
through the gap in the door
I kept my distance
explained my situation
asked if I could use his phone
he didn't have one
but offered to tow me out

we made our way to his car
an old station-wagon
faux wood-panelled sides
the tires almost flat
it wouldn't start
four wheezing coughs
it needed a push he told me
so, I pushed the old station-wagon
almost all the way to the ditch

I could see my car, the nose of it
poking out and up
by the time the station-wagon sputtered to life
I hopped onto the passenger seat
breathless and sweating
to hear his life story

he was English
here 60 years
still had the accent
he had followed love

but, two summers before
cancer had come for love
found love
and taken love away

I had seen other men cry
seen tears in their eyes
tears roll down their face
but, usually, they were silent cries
silent tears
his came roaring
he shook with wails
I did what I could
said what I could
but when he stopped
it was only
because there was nothing
nothing at all
left in him

I looked under the car
secured the rope
climbed onto the driver's seat
gave him the thumbs up
and we both lurched gently forward
inch by inch towards level ground

when it was over the sun had set
but light still made it
from beyond the horizon

I walked to his car window
he didn't get out
bad knees
one replaced already
one due
he told me of his two boys
far flung
one in Auckland
one in Tokyo
told me I reminded him of them

I thanked him
his handshake was firm
we took a last look at each other
he beeped his horn twice as he drove away
it was the only sound for miles

ALCHEMY

Most people are sleeping
purring, dreaming
while I sit here
awake enough to write
too tired to go to bed

the letters on the screen blur and sway
the night presses itself against the kitchen window
my fingers hover above the keys
patient
waiting for instruction

I like the emptiness
just me and the dark and the dancing letters
every breath a secret
the small-hour alchemy of time
turning nothing
into more nothing

WAX

I had become deaf in my left ear
not entirely
just enough to frustrate people
who now had to repeat themselves
loudly

I am getting older but I am not old
not yet
is what I told myself
I went to the doctor
he looked in my ears

wax
just wax and lots of it
he told me to remain still
flooded my ear canal with warm water
it was not unpleasant

he held a small plastic container towards me
wax, and lots of it
I asked him how long the wax might have been there
how long it would have taken to build up
"A long, long time."

I wondered how long
I wondered if there were remnants
miniscule remnants
from the before
from the then

were there traces from my boyhood
from those freewheeling bubble-gum days
from the times in my back-garden tent when you looked at me
and I looked away
trembling

were there cellular fingerprints
a tenuous link to a world of slithering shadows
when I held on by my fingernails
for one hundred thousand minutes
and made it

was there a molecular connection to
I'm sorry
I can't
I'll try
I do

"How does that feel?"
his voice loud, much louder now in my ear
reminding me
that it didn't matter much now
the wax was gone

SURFACE TENSION

So much goes on below
beneath
behind
there are eggshells under the floorboards
there are mice in the walls
there are pulses in my ears
marrow churning in my bones

I read an article about ducks
how eating too much bread causes wing deformity
a wing deformity called "angel wing"
that results in the bird being unable to fly
"*angel wing*"

they have to paddle furiously in the first place
just to swim
and now this

SHE CALLS IT MY PINKIE FINGERNAIL

Right now, it is a soft red colour
with five purple polka dots
yellow glitter
and a shiny gloss coating

I look at her face, just inches from mine
her eyes are nearly crossed
her tongue peeks out between her teeth in concentration
she is plaiting my beard, and I am letting her

she sometimes draws love hearts on my arms and hands
says they are full of love for when she is in school
calls them juicy
I find myself in no hurry to wash them off

she came to me today, wet-eyed, with a worm in her hands
told me it was sick and asked how we could save it
she was sure that I would know
and all of a sudden, I did

SPIDERS HAVE EIGHT EYES

The spider is busy
is always busy
it should relax, take it easy
treat its web as a hammock
lie back, take a breath

I wonder how far
with all of those eyes
it can see

the horizon
the end of the garden
an inch beyond its web

I wonder if it can see the silken beauty
the impossible art hanging
in the space between my wing mirror and the car door
delicate home
glistening death trap

frenzied squirming
web shroud
sucking, hungry fangs
that leave a husk
a hollow tombstone

I wonder if
with all of those eyes
does it see

probably not

WATCHING A FRENCH FILM IN A DUBLIN CINEMA, TWELVE YEARS AGO

Our illuminated faces
two hundred moons
the film was French
subtitled
everyone was laughing
a little too long
don't get me wrong
it was funny
a little
but
not near as funny as the moon faces seemed to think

maybe it was me
maybe I just needed to lighten up
relax
let myself enjoy it
I waited for the next wave
felt the swell of it
watched something mildly funny
laughed as long and as hard as the rest of them
and, just like that
I was an asshole

LONDON

It was our first visit to London
I had expected more
for it to be different
but there it was
old, grey buildings
pasty skinned people shuffling by
the smiles of camera-carrying tourists
the only light
Dublin, with more pigeons

after grabbing a bite to eat
we descended beneath the city
The Tube
that impossible maze of echoing burrows
the smell of rubber, oil and bodies
streams of people
flowing down and down

we arrived at a platform
holding a map with coloured lines
something our daughter might have scribbled
a train was coming
preceded by a charge in the air

the slow rumble exploding
as it roared into our bubble

the train stopped quickly and all the doors flew open at once
a man stepped out
a big man
in a small jacket
the sleeves reaching only halfway down his forearms
he moved in stops and starts
jittering, just yards from us

the train doors closed
a calm and mechanical voice said
Train departing. Please step away from the platform.
within seconds the train was gone
as if it had never been there in the first place
the jittering man looked at me
red-eyed, I saw it dawn on him
"My bag. My bag!"

he ran to the edge of the platform
leaned out
looked into the dark and empty tunnel
and screamed into the thundering silence

UP ON THE WIRE

I liked to throw things
can't explain why
I ended up with a javelin in my hand
but, before that
I threw everything else
stones
snowballs
tennis balls
frisbees
one infinite summer we tied a pair of old shoes together
for me
to throw up on the wire

with my father I would try
to skim stones
from Dollymount
to Hollyhead
I didn't make it
but I got closer than most

my friends and I found a dart one day
glinting by the kerb
we passed it around as a treasure

amazed how someone could lose it
it was speckled with rust
but the body was straight
the flight was perfect
and the point
sharp enough to split an atom

we tossed for who had the first throw
I won
the heft of it in my palm
small, dense and weighty
I put it between my fingers
took a runup
let it go
hard as I could
a perfect throw

we watched it sail up and on
the flight spinning blue and silver
we watched it arc gently down
watched a girl on a bicycle
cycle slowly into its path
she wore shorts
the dart stuck firmly and silently
into her thigh
somehow, she didn't feel it
kept on cycling
the dart, in deep
stuck, perpendicular
unnoticed

until, her friend pointed at it
and I started to run
the dart had covered the distance
in one long second or two short ones
I don't know how long it took me
but I got to her
as she calmly reached down
pulled it out
smiled
handed me the dart
cycled away
there was not one drop of blood

U-TURN

Things are rarely as bad
or as good
as they seem
one minute you are driving
the streetlights pulsing by
music blaring
throat ragged from the singalong
then the phones rings
bad news
the worst news
one U-turn later
the car is silent
the streetlights insipid
the road a salty blur

good is temporary
bad is temporary
everything in between is temporary
every silver lining has a cloud
and summer hides in every snowflake

SEAGULLS AND SILENCE

I wipe sea spray from your fringe
you point to the horizon excitedly
there is nothing
only seagulls and silence
I look back and you are gone

I find you in the kitchen
the kettle whistles
and we let it
we pick the dried candle wax off the table
in a walnut coffee haze until
there is a shriek

and I am running
and she has blood running down her shin
ice cream soaks up tears and she
is running
away, once again
later, we play Monopoly and my father phones
we chat, he tells that he has just watched a film
Gregory Peck was so young

I return to giggles and discover
that I have lost my fortune

we laugh, we laugh and never cry
besides our happy tears
and I can still taste the salt of them
and I can still see you all, the ghosts of you
and I know that I shouldn't go back there
but I do, because only you
only you
can understand

GLASS BOTTOM

I am surrounded by smiles
smiles so wide
I find myself wondering
how the smiling faces
do not crack
allowing what is in
to seep out

we stand on a glass bottomed boat
looking down
and through
the underwater cosmos
I find myself wondering
if the glass were to crack
would we fall through
or would the water come
and find us

SIMMERING

There was always a guy with freakish strength
generally wiry
happy to stay in the background
an easy wallflower
he avoided trouble
dodged first and second glances
but the strength, simmering steel
was always there
utterly disproportionate to his frame

bigger guys bounced off him on pitches
arm wrestles were won smoothly
and without expression
to sighs and disbelief
even deep cuts and gashes never phased him
I didn't know what to put it down to
this defiance of natural laws

always so quiet, so placid
I never knew where the strength came from
until years later
when I learned
that the placid
have more rage than anyone

MASKS

It took them hours
my wife and daughter
to make the masks
I watched them sit at the picnic table
cutting, measuring, sewing
polka-dotting
for half a sunny day

these are the things
that we do now
to stop the spread
it is a new world
a world of masks, of gloves
of distance
and enormous phone bills

the virus cannot reach her here
but she wears it now on the tire swing
and laughs
with her hidden mouth
and I am taken back thirty-five years
when we would pretend to be soldiers
though we never had to go to war

THE CURE

We sing songs now
while washing our hands
over and over, again and again

we draw "tattoos" on our arms
go to bed late, get up late
have our breakfast at lunchtime

we shoot hoops, score goals, play hopscotch
find new places to hide
invent terrible magic tricks

we mix water, salt and vinegar
blackcurrant cordial and a raw egg
my daughter thinks it might be the cure

in bed, our legs twitch questions
keeping us awake
and talking in circles

these empty days are filled
with once forgotten things
and a shrinking world expands

THE UNWRITTEN POEM

I try to write a poem a day
though that doesn't always pan out
sometimes there are more days than poems
sometimes, more poems than days
I had expected, as I sit here at midnight
after a Huckleberry summer day
that the words would have come
gently and easily
with no need for cooing or crowbars
but not tonight
not a chance
as my wife and daughter are sleeping
in a tent outside
I *say* sleeping but
in the last half hour alone they have come inside
to use the toilet, boil the kettle (for hot-water bottles)
get some socks, get some water, turn off the outside lights
they have come inside to tell me about night-time noises
and the cats
and to ask me if I would like a square of chocolate
and to boil the kettle again

to fill a third hot-water bottle
for Lambie, a favourite teddy
who is chilly
apparently

I suppose
that sometimes
the days themselves are poems
I close the laptop
brush my teeth and go to bed

THOUSAND-THREAD-COUNT SHEETS

People say that when they go
they want to go sleeping
they want to put their head
on a goose down pillow
pull thousand-thread-count sheets
in around their necks
and slip, smiling, into a bottomless
warm black lake

we know now that the virus
will leave many of us
to die on hospital beds
alone
listening to an ECG
beep…beep………beep
to silence
many of us will die gasping
for the bright and dizzy breaths
we never ever took
will die with hearts spiralling
in our chests

the way they might have done
but never did

for those of us that remain
the billions
millions
hundreds
dozens
we will need to find our fears
grab them
shake and roar at them
until they are broken, twitching things
then find each other
and give all that we have left

THE POEMS

I would write them
she would read them
that's how it always went
she would read slowly
on her first pass
before, without a word, reading again

she would tell me how they made her feel
where they had succeeded
where they failed
sometimes, her finger would touch the words on the screen
to connect, gain a deeper understanding
or coax some more from them

it was a gradual thing at first
I noticed that she read them just the once
and quickly too
her finger no longer reaching for the words
only the *page down* key
and then she said it

"Nice," the poem was nice
nice

I stayed silent, just in case
but there was no more
she stood up
and poured some pasta into a saucepan

the poems kept on coming
were all read quickly
were all nice
I don't know what changed
what I did know
was that nice was no good to me

so, I held them back
kept them to myself
she didn't ask
she doesn't ask
and I thought that I had won
but now, I'm not so sure

VEGETABLES AND IRON

He was waiting for me
behind the school gate pillar
he came from behind
grabbed me in a headlock
I didn't know who he was
just felt the rough green of his parka jacket on my cheek
we tussled
in peculiar silence
he smelled of vegetables and iron
I pushed against him
sending us into a wall
he forced the top of my head across it
I felt the sound of it
the heat of it
then, it was over
I watched him walk away
an older boy, two years up
bright red hair, spring in his step
I didn't even think to ask why

SOME DAYS

Blood matted his hair and covered his face
strewn about his feet were black feathers
and pieces of crows that he had torn asunder
the worst was his smile
white and pure
anyone's smile

I opened my eyes
awake and away
from him, and it all
I sharpened my ear
held it out like a knife
silence, nothing

I dressed myself
stripped the bed
boiled the kettle
took the coffee
in my nose and on my tongue
got lost in the quartz of the black kitchen worktop

I hung the sheets on the washing line
white and pure against the autumn

hoping the rain would hold off
the phone rang
I let it
a dog barked somewhere

she came home trumpeting the horn
bringing the weekend with her
we brought the sheets in
and some of the day with them
we made the bed and lay upon it
the day was half full, and half empty

I stretched my arm towards the ceiling
let my hand go limp
she asked me a question but before I could answer
she punched my shoulder, laughing
pointed down at my feet
the heels of my shoes had left two crescents of mud
some days that's just how things go

COBBLESTONES

I didn't think that I had lost my way
the buildings were the usual
old, granite edged, their quartz glint long dulled
the cobblestones uneven as always
soft cornered
hard worn by people long gone
and those long gone before them

I walked with ghosts
and their eyes looked through me just the same
it was only when I walked through the archway
down the steps
saw the river
wide and rainbowed with oil
that I realised
I had never been here before

TICKS AND TOCKS

She can't tell the time
not yet
I have tried to teach her
but my heart was not in it
I'm not sure she needs to know
not yet
time
the most human of constructs
can do what it does best

hide in shadowed doorways
sit on frozen sunrays

lie underneath the lawn
sleep beyond the dawn

time

can wait

BAKER'S LOUNGE, VICAR STREET, FIFTEEN YEARS AGO

The air had a tang to it
a sticky, almost viscous tang
it coated the back of my throat as I sucked it down
the buses were on strike
I was stranded in Dublin
but it was alright
the purgatory of the office was behind me
the evening, grey and heavy, was mine

I wandered, without purpose, as always
a hungry snake, I was charmed into a chipper
by salt and vinegar music
the sizzle of the oil
my stomach leaping into a Pavlovian breakdance
the brown paper hot in my hands
stinging steam rising upwards
forever, forever

I listened to the news in a café
no breakthrough in the bus strike

they wanted more money
better hours
me too
the world went by
I let it
it was alright

I hate pubs, the forced laughter
the lubricated bonhomie
but, Ireland were playing on the telly
and I wanted to see it
I took a breath, pushed in the door
let the clinking staleness wash over me
all men
all old

all eyes were on the big screen
I walked to the bar
waited
I have a superpower
I become invisible in pubs
the teams were lining up
the crowd was simmering
I waited

"What can I get you?"
"Just a Coke thanks."
he shook his head
I watched his disdain ramp up to contempt
"Here you go, just-a-Coke."

I sat away from the old men
the floor was sticky
the Coke was flat

the national anthems began, first the Spanish
the old men swore and swayed and booed
I sucked on my Coke, glad of my superpower
the announcer said, solemnly
"And now for the Irish national anthem, Abhrán na bhFiann."
the old men stood up, ramrod straight
put their hands on their hearts
I noticed the upward tilt of their chins

some closed their eyes, one removed his cap
they sung from their stomachs and their chests
not knowing the words, I remained silent
almost chewing the neck of the Coke bottle
staying invisible
holding my breath
when I heard it
quietly at first

somebody was singing "God Save the Queen"
instinctively, I looked at the door
three strides away from me
I could be out in just a couple of seconds
my body steeled itself
I was ready
the singing got louder
I looked at the old men, they had fallen silent

from in among them, one voice
"Loooong live our noooooble queen!"
louder
"Send her victooooorious!"
louder still
"Haaaappy and glooooorious!"
at the top of his voice
"God saaaaave the queeeeeen!"

I saw him, rising up from the centre of them
the words boiling, pouring from him
rippling the air with their heat
he stepped from them then
caught eyes with me
oblivious to my superpower
smiled
stood upon a chair
"Confound their politics!"
"Get down off the chair Benji!"
"Frustrate their knavish tricks!"
"Come on Benji, down you get."
"Long may she reign!"
"Jesus Benji would you stop, fucking, singing!"
he stepped onto a table
"God saaaave us all!"

he looked at me then, winked
raised his glass
to me

oh no
everyone turned, looked toward me
my knuckles whitened
I wondered if the Coke bottle might shatter in my hand
Abhrán na bhFiann crescendoed to a finish
there was silence

Benji, standing precariously on the table
turned back to the old men, to the barman
raised his glass again, and shouted
in an accent so Dublin,
he might have descended from Molly Malone herself
"Youse are nothing but a shower of wankers!"
more silence
then, the whistle blew, the match started
and I watched Benji disappear

JUST TO DRIVE

We weren't friends exactly
not acquaintances either
somewhere in between
still, I visited him once
in prison

he seemed fine
the same
we chatted, this and that
the old days
the new days
what it was like

he told me that it was alright
the inmates were fine
the guards were fine
it was alright
he told me that the hardest part
was how, sometimes, he looked for his car keys
hoping to head out
just to drive
how, sometimes, he reached for his cigarettes
his lips tingling

to find his pocket empty
how, sometimes, late at night he made plans
absentminded plans
for the next day
the next week
the next year

THE HIGH COST OF BREATHING

The sign threw me at first
"The Oxygen Bar"
after a cartoon doubletake
I stepped inside
eager to know
would it be
could it be
it was

a dozen people sat at the bar
smiling under oxygen masks
breathing pure air
scented with flowers and butterscotch
cinnamon and sea
€10 for ten minutes
a euro a minute
I looked at my watch
walked back out
the Dublin wind struck my cheek with an open palm
it was a wild day

BLACKBERRIES

She would not lie on her hospital bed
didn't feel sick
felt the same
the same as ever
her voice shrill, sharp and urgent
we talked as we always did
as if there were no tubes
running in
running out of her
she sipped a cup of tea
wasn't hungry
a good thing
as to eat
was to feed what was in her

while taking her womb
they found three tumours
cut them out
lay her back on her bed
a six-day coma
when she woke, she asked for her car keys
she spoke as if there was sand in her throat
her voice suddenly old, slow

the next day she told me
that she feels sick now
that it hurts to cough
to speak
to move
to breathe

I walked past her garden today
the blackberries rot on the branch, unpicked

REINCARNATION

She came up with the theory of reincarnation
by herself
she is seven-years-old
I listened to her calmly tell me
that maybe when we die
we leave ourselves
to come again as a lizard or a bird
or even a tree
as trees are living, breathing things too

it made sense to her
and halfway, to me
so, I let her keep it
didn't contradict her
because, after all
what do I know?

later that evening
while she wriggled to sleep in her bed
I thought of religion
I considered how
if their foundations can be born
in the mind of a seven-year-old
well, they absolutely must be wrong
or right

"HAVE YOU GOT A MINUTE?"

My mother is on the phone
she needs to talk
about the weather
but
not really about the weather
it comes, eventually
she has been thinking about a conversation we had on Sunday
it has been haunting her
she hopes that she didn't upset me
that she didn't say something she shouldn't have
I can barely remember it
we talk about it all the same
I reassure her
talk to her as she once talked to me
tell her that she worries too much
that she shouldn't care what people think of her anyway
the phone is silent
before she asks
"Do you really think so?"

BLANK AND EMPTY

I had heard the bang
a firecracker
one of many
thought nothing of it
the team had won
we were on the street outside the stadium
car horns blared
the air was dense with chanting
holy jubilation
I felt him turn towards me
his face, blank and empty
his eyes, wondering
his right hand grasped his left wrist
he presented it to me, his left hand
or what remained of it
most of it was gone
his palm was missing
his thumb was missing
one of his fingers
part of one of his fingers, flapped
boneless, downward
the others, gone
his hand, what was left of it

hung, open and red
meat, just meat
exposed
to the breeze and exhaust fumes
hanging from him
uselessly
I looked back up
his face, blank and empty still
I don't know why
I reached to cup it
he never made a sound

HE DIDN'T MAKE IT

I had been thinking about him
remembering the good and bad old days
the maths teacher had thrown a duster at him once
he had caught it and thrown it back
that quiet fire
the chalk remained on the teacher's shoulder for the rest of the day
a ghost's handprint

we were different and the same
in ways
years after school I met him on the bus
both of us drenched from the rain
he was the same, but different

I bumped into his brother today
told him how I had been trying to get in touch
his face was ash
he had died
just last week
he didn't tell me how
and I didn't ask

BOTTOM LINES AND DEADLINES

I remember my last day
the day I got the hell out of there
the day that I escaped
finally
from the meetings and bureaucracy
bottom lines and deadlines
from being called
"a resource"
I remember walking through the lobby
running
running
to the car
I remember not looking back
I know they thought me crazy
to leave a steady job
to have no job lined up
no safety net
I know they thought me crazy
maybe they were right
but they are still there
and I
am not

THE ARAN CARDIGAN

The heat is on in the house
yet he sits in his armchair
with a small fan-heater beside him
his own personal sun

we wear t-shirts
and overheat still
the house
so warm
that the curtains stick to the windows
he wears layers upon layers
a vest, a shirt, a jumper
his old, worn, Aran cardigan

I remember the first time I saw him wear it
how it occurred to me that he was old
maybe even mortal
it fitted him then
it hangs on him now
faded and shapeless
he tells me that he can't get the heat into him
tells me that it must be that damn Warfarin
that, and other things

he remembers summer heat on his skin
the feel of it
the *feel* of it
he didn't know that it was something he could miss
so much

days at the beach
afternoons when perspiration blossomed
salty flowers blooming
from young and fertile skin
he remembers himself
a stack of calendars ago
an old friend
left behind

THE CEILING

At first, I thought that I was dying
I felt a pull
an upward pull
from my shoulders initially
then my chest
I looked down to see my feet
slightly off the floor
I hung there, in wonder
wondering what might happen next
slowly, steadily I rose
weightless
or, lighter than air at least
I reached
was caught by
the ceiling

for several minutes I lay there
enjoying the feeling
I never thought to move
never thought to push myself off
I just lay there
on my back
on the ceiling

my whole world upside down

I fell eventually of course
landing shoulder first with a thump
I felt the press of gravity again
the gentle crush
knowing that nobody would believe me
I made a coffee
took in the aroma deep as I could
and looked up at the ceiling
a thousand miles away

HOT CHOCOLATE

She told me that her wishes are coming true
For real Dad!
that she knew that our cat, Boots, was lonely
so, she wished
hard
for a cat pal for him and the very next day
one came
(a stray)
she named George
who is special
Because he is made from a wish

she told me that when her teacher needed a helper
she closed her eyes
so hard the dark went bright
and wished and wished and wished until
He chose me Dad! He chose me!

she told me that just yesterday she wished
for ten minutes
Or even more!
for a hot chocolate
then, in the evening her mother made her one

The most delicious one ever! Just like I wished for!
I put my hands on her shoulders
and told her
that hot chocolate wishes always come true

SOMETIMES YOU'VE JUST GOT TO LAY DOWN THE LAW

His voice booms across the road
he slips, behind it, smiling, between the traffic
we shake hands
he is a man
a real man
confident, in control
I am a man
but not a real man

he talks
tells me about his sons
how talented they are
how the girls love them
how they have inherited so much from him
I listen, hear
how happy he is
how happy they are
now

they are getting the house done up again
the window guy was messing him around
but it is all sorted now
sometimes you've just got to lay down the law
speak to them in ways they can understand
I find myself nodding

perfunctorily
he asks how things are with me
hurries me through my answers
great-great-great
offers his hand again
tells me that I need to lose weight
that it was great to see me
really great-great-great

he turns
I watch him walk away
feeling a hell of a lot more
than ten minutes older

I remember once, he stood behind me on Grafton Street
while I withdrew £300
from a bank machine
he could barely look me in the eye
almost bowed as he took it
promised he would pay me back
the first chance he could

WHY I DON'T READ THE NEWSPAPERS

I read about him in the newspaper
apparently, the other guy had looked his woman
up and down
whatever that meant
he probably didn't expect the punch
probably didn't see it coming
it was enough

while unconscious the other guy
with a small pocket scissors
cut his eyelids off
he told the judge that he did it
"So that he could never stop looking"
whatever that meant

he got eight years
will probably serve two
I believe the libraries in prisons are excellent
and in the yard
if he looks up
the clouds will be as beautiful to him
as to me

DUSK

Dusk had fallen softly and in secret
only a sliver of the day remained
melting onto the horizon
bedtime was coming

drowsy fairies lay on her eyelids
her deepening breaths a lullaby
"I feel a bit sad Dad and I don't know why."
I am still amazed how my whole heart
can fit in the palm of her hand

I smile at her
she smiles back
her cheeks are warm and rosy
I open my arms and in she comes
the heat of her pouring
through thin pyjamas

I carry her to her bedroom window
open the curtains
her eyes widen
scattering fairies
"Look at the colours!
Even at night!"

SEEING MY TEACHER AT THE SAVOY CINEMA, DUBLIN IN 1983

My father's hand
huge and tough-skinned
holding mine
I remember letting it go
when I saw her

we stood on the red velvet lake
queuing in a hot popcorn haze
she stood across from me
not the same
her lips, blood red and smiling
her hair, down, longer than I would have imagined
she wore a skirt
I saw her calves
her knees
the beginnings of her thighs
she was with a man

I saw his hand move about her waist
her back, her hip
I saw him lean in
watched his mouth brush her ear
mysterious whispers
she flung her head back
her neck, white and wild and soft
I had never heard her laugh
not like that

we caught eyes
something passed between us
and I knew
then
that she was real
and maybe
she knew
at last
that I was too

THE HANDYMAN

He came to fix the shower
and install a back-garden light
his breath, warm in the winter air
lit as rising steam in the porchlight

screwdrivers hung from his toolbelt
weapons of a Kildare apache
he talked about wiring
voltages
the fuse-box
I nodded and tutted at the appropriate times
fooling nobody

he told me of the time he landed in hospital
close to death
having breathed in a cocktail of sawdust and paint fumes
I thought of paper cuts and the time I stapled my thumb

he talked of drinking and fistfights
drank his coffee
one gulp to start, another to finish
and jumped into his van
off to install a radiator for someone
I waved him off and walked to the kitchen to unload the dishwasher

THESE THINGS WILL KILL ME

He lit a cigarette
took a drag
closed his eyes
savouring
these things will kill me
he exhaled, an easy smile
I looked at him
made a myth by the smoke
sunshine on his shoulders
not caring about tomorrow
and all the tomorrows to come
little did he know
that he would live forever
or whatever passes
for forever
nowadays

EAMONN

He sat at the bank of desks next to mine
he had some strange verbal ticks
would hum
gently
after each sentence
it was disconcerting
he would also sigh
long and loudly
before each sentence
he was an odd guy

his work was fine
professional on the phone
efficient on the computer
fine
one day his desk was empty
I thought nothing of it
it stayed empty for the week
I asked around
nobody knew a thing

my boss approached me
asked me if I had heard from him

as I seemed to be the only person that he talked to
she had tried to contact him to no avail
another two weeks passed
with no sighing or humming

it came to a month
he had not responded to phone calls
emails
even letters
so, my boss drove to the address he had given
knocked at the door
a lady answered
she did not know anyone by his name
having lived in the house ten years

I arrived in work the next day
his desk was no longer empty
a smiling young woman in a red jumper stood up and shook my hand
she had no verbal ticks
my boss referred to her as “a go-getter”
she would be better than fine

the following summer I ended up sitting beside him on the bus
I began to talk to him
but he pretended not to know me

DESTINATION RESTAURANT

I had never heard the term before
until I read it in an online review
it refers to a remote restaurant
quaint, somewhat bizarre in its location
somewhere you will not come upon naturally
but must journey to specifically

destination restaurants should have outstanding food
to make the trip worthwhile
this one must
as it is full
despite not being in the *middle* of nowhere
but on the very edge
my stomach grumbles but it is not the only sound

I had never really considered the word 'guffaw' before
I may have never really heard a guffaw before
I imagined loud, joyous, jolly laughter
infectious, smile inducing laughter
the table next to us guffaws
as if in competition

it is…unpleasant

a guffaw is a toothy laugh
think of a truffle scoffing, oily-mouthed snob
or a horse on acid
I look at them, guffawing on and on
and wonder if they realise
just how lucky they are
that I have let them live

NEW YEAR'S EVE 2019

We stumble
ready to fall
into another year
another decade

I ask my father if he is looking forward to 2020
he is quiet
I wait
"Sure, I suppose so."

we walk to the garage under the sky
flecked with mute winter birds
he looks for masonry nails
"I can't find anything anymore."

he is always cold now
so, I have painted him the sun
to give him warmth
or the illusion of warmth at least

I try to hang it over the mantelpiece
he insists on helping, "Many hands make light work."
I notice the butt of a pencil behind his ear

I am a boy again

he scrapes a little paint away with his rule
"I can't do anything right anymore."
unaware that I prefer it
now that it has become a collaboration

in the evening he asks me
if I am looking forward to 2020
I think about it
"Sure, I suppose so."

DISASSEMBLING

Somebody had thought to cover his knee
before he could see it
I had seen it
the mess of it
the utter disassembling of it
as he lay on his back
too stunned to move
I kneeled beside him
while somebody called for an ambulance

he looked at me, blinking questions
tried to get up
I shook my head
we talked as we waited
he was not in any pain
I suggested that it might be the shock
he said, *the shock of what?*

he asked if the ambulance was for him
asked if it was bad
I said yes
and yes
he tried to get up again

I put my hand on his chest
felt the beat and the heat of his heart

we were quiet for a while
I noticed that I was holding his hand
he gazed up at the clouds
I heard a siren
distant
strangely ominous
I hoped that it would take its time

MISSISSIPPI MUD PIE

Here we are again
me, trying not to let him notice
that I am looking to escape
him, talking and talking and talking
and talking
he tells me that people find him entertaining
I wouldn't mind
at all
if he went to find those people

he tells me how he has had his fair share of women
more than his fair share in fact
how people feared him on the pitch
and off it
how he will be rich this time next year
or the year after
at the latest
how he can drink any man
or woman!
under the table

he tells me of his holidays
his property abroad

the famous people he has met
and entertained
how he has dozens of designer shirts unworn
how his daughter is going to qualify
first in her class from medical school
how she might be the one
to finally crack that awful cancer business once and for all

I am required only to nod and laugh
although I wonder
if he knows that he is talking to a man
who once ate a sixteen slice
Mississippi mud pie
alone
in one sitting
as if it was nothing

I DON'T SMOKE

Over halfway there
some time left
but every passing year brings with it
more chance
of the doc sighing
fixing me in his gaze
breaking *the* news
asking me if I am alright
when he has just told me otherwise

I don't know how I will react
but I do know that before the end
I will buy a pack of cigarettes
perfect the opening
lighting
holding
I will lean against a wall
the sun setting behind me
take a drag, let it go
cool, for once
as curls of smoke
rise up
forever

REGULAR JOE

We sat beside each other
watching the shuttlecock arc
quickly up
slowly down
perfect, delicate grace
utterly at odds with the leaping grunts of the players

he leaned into me
told me in a hush
that he played the game once
that watching
is not the same but
it's all that he can do now

an older guy
wearing older-guy clothes
he leaned into me again
told me that his shoulder was gone
that his hip needed replacing
that he had represented Ireland all over the world

had played in the Olympics
had mingled with elite athletes and dignitaries
but now, was just a regular Joe
sitting in an old school hall in Edenderry, County Offaly
beside a man
who didn't have a thing to say

THE ROLEX

It was a Rolex
I didn't believe him at first
but there it was
he blew the dust away
dust sixty years dormant
alive again, and pluming by the window

I had never seen one before
not in real life
I had to squint to see
R-o-l-e-x
I thought back to my childhood
he had worked so long and so hard
and we had everything
but, they weren't Rolex days

I imagined him
young and vibrant
his shock of hair
pitch black and Brylcreemed
days before so much
days before me
his Rolex days

long since left behind

the Rolex no longer worked
he had tried to get it fixed
to discover that sometimes parts for old things
are no longer available
he tells me that he will leave it to me
he smiles
I can't smile back

ONE MORE WEEK

She is seven years old
for one more week
she listens to Carmen McRae sing 'Take Five'
recorded with Dave Brubeck
in 1961
when the horizon was empty
of both of us

she wrote a poem in the summertime
'Popcorn Clouds'
about my father being lonely
having read it
I was quiet
while I waited
for the lump in my throat to subside

when I was seven years old
I put a staple in the pad of my thumb
so deep
that I could see the prongs
pressed against the underside of my nail
I pulled it out with my teeth
spat it into the bathroom sink

she is seven years old
for one more week
and then
she will be eight

AND THE REST

There will come a day
when everyone has been forgotten
Salinger, Beethoven, Einstein
Jesus, Buddha, Mohammad
and the rest
maybe then
we will realise
that even immortality
is short lived

A SPECK AGAINST THE SUN

As is so often the case
I thought it was a weed at first
the shoot, almost translucent
emerging
somehow
from a crack in the cement

each morning, while crunching on cereal
I watched it stay alive
not die
but grow
barely and barely
from the crack

as late spring heat found it
it became stronger
braver
taller
before, one morning
a bud

a week of cereal was crunched
then colour, from cement
yellow tipped
burning red
fire
somehow

springtime passed in secret
the warmth of summer came
I ate my breakfast outside
the stem was thick
the two leaves, outstretched
the petals glowed

on the last morning I sat
watched it grow before my eyes
just a little
watched it lift out of the crack
move gently upwards
I watched it rise
craned my neck
as it became a speck against the sun
tried not to blink until it was gone
looking back
the thing that I remember most
was the perfect silence of it all

THE CHALLENGE

I
challenged
myself
to
write
a
poem
with
just
one
word
on
each
line

I
have
come
close
several
times
but
always
seem
to
fall
at
the
final hurdle

THE MURDERER

He had hailed me to wish a happy new year
I rolled down the passenger window
letting in a wet January breeze
he stooped, rested his elbows
leaned in, ready to chat

we spoke of our Christmases
how we saw one decade become another
before he began to talk
and talk
about what interested him most
murder
and those who commit them

he had watched programs and films
read newspapers and books
fascinated by the mechanics of it all
eager to discover what drove people to murder
the bloody details of the act itself
the mistakes that they had made
that led to their capture

he had known two murderers himself
timid men
still in prison
he assured me that they were gentlemen
though he had washed his hands of both

I wondered aloud if the capacity to murder
given the right set of circumstances
was in us all
he looked at me with fresh eyes
horrified
said, "No," quickly and definitively
as an innocent hour
lay broken and twitching on the muddy road between his feet

2019

He says it was a long while ago
back in 2002
and I think
that wasn't too long ago
before remembering
that it is not 2009 now
but 2019
with 2020
coming hard and fast

when I was a boy, I was sure, that by 2020
we would have hover cars
four-course meals compressed into a pill
robots everywhere

when I was a boy, I was sure, that by 2020
we would at least
have figured out
how not to be
so awful
to each other

THE LOCAL PEOPLE AT THE LOCAL TENNIS CLUB

You have never seen such rain
bouncing high, watery fireworks
from the sizzling ground
we played on all the same
our mixed-doubles match
nearing its end

people watched from the clubhouse
my wife and daughter among them
though someone had a special eye on them
had been chipping away for months
snide remarks, petty stuff
we had let it go
got on with things
kept on hitting the ball

until that night
when my wife and daughter
were told to leave
were told that our daughter was too young

was not allowed to be there
that the 9.00pm threshold had come and gone
the clock having struck 9.01pm

she had barrelled past other minors
other children not watching their fathers
finish out their games
who were allowed to stay on
until 9.02pm and beyond

we left
did not go back
she remains, clenching the reins of her high horse
even sent a text
I'm so very sorry
        for being right
the chairman called
tried to get us back
but we weren't for tennis
and tennis wasn't for us
he told me
that the main thing is
that we knew
it was nothing personal
I told him
that it absolutely was
there was nowhere else to go
after that

REGGAE

Some of my favourites have tried it
broken away from themselves
recorded and released a reggae song
or, as Kate Bush once said
"a song *infused* with reggae."
the results are a kind of aural poison
a chimeric sonic abomination
the musical equivalent of a cold pint
of vomit and razorblades

reggae should be left to the experts
those who record and release reggae
for a living
although
even to those
I would implore
please don't

THE GOOD OLD DAYS

I watch the twinkle in his eye return
as he talks about the good old days
the days when they had nothing
or next to nothing
and were happy with it
the days when he made mischief
with pals long since gone
how they took their clips round the ear
because they deserved it
how the meat had a taste
how his mother made the gravy just right
how you could leave your front door open
how when he saw her that night in the dancehall
he just knew
I watch the twinkle in his eye dance
when he says
"Things were better then."

not having been there
I agree, all the same
while knowing
that things weren't better then
not at all
it is just
that they are worse today

HE HAD BEEN TIRED RECENTLY, A LITTLE SHORT OF BREATH

There was a thorough post-mortem
as he had been a young man
as young and old as I am
cancer
cancer from head to toe
riddled
is what they would say in the pub that evening

I skipped the pub
slipped away straight after
taking my memories with me
I walked through the puddles
let the water wet my socks
just to feel something
something else

on the train home I wondered why he didn't have any pain
he had been tired recently
a little short of breath
I went back a few years
to his kitchen, when she said
with a wink
what he doesn't know won't kill him

H-A-P-P-Y

She made me a pendant today
silver letters, silver charms
on a strip of soft, black leather
a daisy, a football and
H-A-P-P-Y
"You are happy Daddy aren't you?"
"Very."
I watch her grow an inch before my eyes

she had pleaded to stay up until midnight
to see one year become another
as if by magic
to sing *that* song
the one that is both happy, and sad
I was sure that she would fade
but midnight came and she stood up
to count down
"10! 9! 8! 7! 6! 5!"
she raised her hands into the air
twirled on the spot once
just because
"4! 3! 2! 1! Happy New Year!"

I didn't think that she knew
the words to Auld Lang Syne
but she did
and as I listened to her I realised
it is not a song for seven-year-olds
too much pathos
I wished for it to end
and then it did
and that was that

ten minutes later she looked up at me from her pillow
we were quiet
her smile was gentle
her blinks were soft and heavy
I squeezed her hand goodnight
in the shadows I couldn't see her lips move
but I heard a slow, slow whisper
"You are happy Daddy aren't you?"
"Very."

THE FOREST IN CHINA WITH NO BIRDS

The one downside
of window seats
is that you are easily trapped

it was a normal bus journey
my forehead vibrated steadily against the glass
we cut through Drumcondra
Dublin City behind us
fifteen minutes from home
when he sat down beside me

he took up all of his seat
and some of mine
great
then, he started talking
as if he were a saucepan boiling over
here we go

the nudges came first
though he never once looked at me
he talked and talked

boiled and boiled
I agreed and agreed

he mentioned King Arthur and Maid Marion
the old carpet shop where his father had worked
a forest in China with no birds
how he used to make his own lead soldiers
how his mother died in a fire
the many uses for old bubble-gum

in amongst it all he made sense
utter, perfect sense
saying, to no one at all
it is easy to be born
even easier to die
what comes between
is the hard part
the bus drove on

BRANCHES

It was just a sapling when we first arrived
before it stretched up
and out
a giant mushroom against the setting sun
a tyre swing hanging from a bough
a fairy door on its trunk
large granite rocks nestling against the base
flowers winding through

I stand underneath it sometimes
almost hidden by the drooping branches
and look up at a glass sky
shattered into ten thousand pieces
by those branches
branches so desperate
for isolation
from themselves
that they fork and fork
and fork again
only to discover
the more that they escape
the less alone they are

THE SPARROWHAWK

The sparrowhawk looked up at me
its eyes, a jarring cartoon yellow
I looked down at it, unsure
we stayed like that
looking at each other
for whole minutes

slowly, I knelt down
gently, I reached for it
it didn't recoil
didn't seem to mind
I took it in my hands
light as its feathers

its small heart fluttered against my palm
a panicked butterfly
I checked one wing
then the other
the first was good, strong
flight ready
the second was limp
the fine bones dust

I wondered what had happened
wondered if a bird could just decide to stop flying
fold its wings against itself at 1000 feet
and fall
and fall
and fall

the sparrowhawk looked over my shoulder
the empty sky
out of reach
for both of us
the sparrowhawk did not know
what was going to happen next
and
neither
did I

THE DANCE CLASS

I come for the last ten minutes
she smiles at me in the floor-to-ceiling mirror
I smile back and cannot stop
my foot taps
my head bobs
her little frame whirls and twirls
jumps and jolts and jerks

she is one of many
some let the music inhabit them
run through them from the ground up
they are surrounded by invisible sparks
there is an effortless lightness

Robin does not quite have it
where they are limber liquid
part of the pulse
my little girl is corners
a blur of elbows
reacting, not feeling
searching, not always finding

sometimes she holds fast onto a passing beat
rides the wave for a few moments
and I am reminded
that magic is a real thing after all
but these moments come
and these moments go
only the joy is constant

but

inside her chest there are no corners
her blood
and some of mine
dark fire dancing
and dancing and dancing
perfectly, wondrously in time
with the only music that really matters

THE BARBER AND THE LIGHTHOUSE

She was cutting my hair
all eight years of her
standing on a chair behind me
scissors in hand

she was taking it very seriously
no small talk with this barber
only snip, snip
snip, snip

small clumps of hair fell
past my ears
landing on my neck and shoulders
snip, snip, snip

she was humming
I asked her a big question
"What is the best thing about life?"
the humming stopped

the snipping didn't
a small answer
"Living."
she asked me a big question in return

"What is the point of life Dad?"
the hair kept falling
the snips kept snipping
I didn't know

"Sometimes in life we are the ocean.
Sometimes we are the lighthouse.
The point of life is to be on the boat."
the snipping stopped

easy silence
"Dad?"
"Yes?"
"You are crazy."

ALMOST

It had been thirty-five years
but there she was
hidden, almost

I saw time on her
two tattoos
one on her wrist
one on the back of her neck
both faded
fad*ing*

I saw the loose thread
the frayed cuffs
her hands, long fingered, elegant
shaking

three times in that hour
she stepped outside
with no explanation
I watched her through the grubby window
standing in the rain
still as she could be
smoking cigarettes

staring hard
at the ground beneath her

she didn't look for shelter
just stood there
in the rain
getting wet
bringing the smell of it with her
each time she came back inside

she didn't say much
neither did I
and in the silence
the clock got louder

and louder
but we ignored
the ticks and the tocks
and their small
tireless teeth
that bite and bite and bite
because there was nothing else that we could do

THE FLAMES AND ASHES OF JOHN DOYLE

You were odd from the start
laughing behind your hands
hands that could speak with a pencil in them
in ways your mouth could not
I remember how you called me odd
how I punched you
how you punched me back, smiling
two oddballs on The North Strand
Dublin, sixty years ago

I heard a fox cub cry last night
I hadn't thought of you for years
but there it was, your mother's scream
that we heard, two doors down
you had gone to the outhouse at the foot of your garden
doused yourself with petrol
struck a match

I saw the smoke from my back garden
but I didn't know, not then
I wonder if there was regret

if you tried to pat the flames away
while you, and part of me, extinguished

at the funeral there was an urn
I don’t know if the ashes smelled of petrol
I don't know where they were scattered
I don’t suppose it matters now

EARLY THURSDAY MORNING, AUTUMN, DUBLIN CITY

On the way to work I walked past a pub
there was a man outside
bent over, hands on his knees
retching, vomiting
again and again
watery
yellowy
and lots of it
steaming in the autumn air
my father once called an early morning pub
The home of the lost

after work I walked to my bus stop
stood in the queue and waited
through the pluming fog of my breath
the city was a Hammer Horror set
across the Liffey, there was a church
the bell was ringing
people filed in
to kneel, to worship
away from music and moonlight
and the whole spinning world
I wondered
what my father would say
to that

THE GULLY

It was hidden
behind vines and hawthorn bushes
it would have gone unnoticed if it weren't for Bob
spying an unexploded firework in the shadowed verge

we crawled along at first
but the dry summer mud was hard on our knees
so, we scraped along on our bellies
two young soldiers behind enemy lines
communicating with nods and coded whispers

I cut my arm on an old tin can
it was painless, the cut being thin and pure
I held my arm up and we watched the blood
roll slowly down my forearm
reach my elbow
fall as plump drops onto, and into, the gully floor

Bob found a silver Hershey wrapper
we had never seen one before
he said *candy* in an American accent
I said it back to him
with a smile he put it in his pocket
to show his brother

we crawled on, brave commandos
dusty and dirty
sweaty and bloody
coming to a small lump of chewing gum

it looked fresh
worth investigating
I prodded it with a stick
it unravelled
a snakeskin
was our first guess
before it took shape
we had never seen a condom before

eventually we came upon a rise
bellied up it to find our faces level with the road
the cars, cruising by
nothing to us, ordinarily
became mysterious things
oblivious to our presence and
we could have grabbed the ankles
of the people walking past
we heard snippets of conversations
not meant for our ears
and once, a lady, a mad lady
walked by talking angrily to herself

nowadays, once in a while
I drive past the gully
and always take a look
hoping to see the whites of eyes
one set
or two
or three
but
there are none

DEAD HEAT IN APRIL

He hadn't changed much in twenty years
I had
though his lie was appreciated
we stood beside our cars
on the petrol station forecourt
talked about the weather at first
how the heat sat on us
dead, with that dead heat smell
what an April

he had gotten married
no kids
his mother had died
I had known
had found out after the funeral
had never gotten in touch
I apologised
he took it
still a better man than me

I told him that we had driven by each other once
that I had stopped my car
jumped out, engine idling

chased him up the road
waving and shouting
until his van stopped
and the window rolled down
and it wasn't him
and it was barely me

he laughed lightly
I shook my head
looked down
damn it was hot
an April like no other
and for a minute more
maybe two
we shot
what little breeze that there was left to shoot

PAGE 86

The sky was huge today
clouds rippled it
interrupting the sunrays as they passed
I sat below
a book propped up on my knees
a still, early summer day

it just appeared, the fly
twitching at the top of page 86
it was unusual
four thin, veined wings
deep red, metallic body
that caught the light

I'm not sure why it chose my book
or why it landed at all
I don't know where it came from
or where it went
if it had something to do
or somewhere to be

I spent thirty seconds or so
thinking about the fly
that twitched at the top of page 86
I wonder if it noticed me at all
probably not
which was fair enough

NAIL CLIPPERS

I cracked the big toenail
on my left foot
doing keepie-uppies, barefoot
in the back garden

I searched the bathroom cabinet
found two pairs of scissors
a nose-hair clipper
two bottles of aftershave
a small tub of omega-3 capsules
some stray cotton buds
an empty box of plasters
some hair bobbins
and a bottle of Star Wars mouthwash

I did not find the nail clippers

I walked to the kitchen
asked my wife if she had seen them
she told me to try the bathroom cabinet
I told her that I had
she returned twenty seconds later
with the nail clippers in her hand

Did you even look in the cabinet?
How can you never find anything?
Honestly, did you look?
It was right there, literally the first thing on the shelf.
You're unbelievable, how did you not see it?
Tell me that you didn't look.

the sun was hot on my neck
the grass, soft under my feet
the ball, comforting, reassuring
on the bridge of my feet
over and over again

ten minutes later
I cracked the big toenail
on my right foot
walked back inside to look for the nail clippers
it wasn't in the kitchen
it wasn't in the bathroom cabinet
I'm sure it'll turn up

360 DEGREES

It had been nothing to me once
but
it turns out
thirty years
is thirty years

my daughter, with her little foot
pushed her new skateboard towards me
it coasted along the tarmac
as, in the pit of my stomach
creaking butterflies dusted themselves off
"Show me a trick Dad."

I thought I would start easy
a three-sixty
thirty summers earlier
I could do three in a row
spinning quick and smooth
tilted back on two wheels
rubber boned and fearless

I stepped onto the board
bent my knees a touch

looked at her
smiled
and
for half a moment
felt invincible again

there was no blue in the sky
just so many different whites
a few patterned greys
some darkness to the east
it took a few seconds
for air to flood my lungs again
in the waiting
I felt the weight of myself
flat on the tarmac
felt what I knew to be blood
run down my knee

my daughter's face appeared
as if from the sky
looked down and asked me
why I was laughing

THE FIGHT

When the time comes
and I am pulled from the fight
I know
I know now
that I will shake my head
hold up my fists
and say
that I am just getting started

Steve Denehan lives in Kildare, Ireland with his wife Eimear and daughter Robin. He is the author of two chapbooks and two collections. Two-time winner of Irish Times' New Irish Writing, his numerous publication credits include Poetry Ireland Review, Acumen, Westerly, and Into The Void. He has been nominated for Best of the Net, Best New Poet, and has been twice nominated for The Pushcart Prize.

www.ingramcontent.com/pod-product-compliance
Lightning Source LLC
LaVergne TN
LVHW010104170826
845678LV00012B/2240

* 9 7 8 1 7 3 8 2 7 3 4 8 5 *